PAINTINGS
from the
CLYDESDALE BANK
COLLECTION

Patrick Bourne

MAINSTREAM
PUBLISHING

First published in Great Britain in 1990 by
MAINSTREAM PUBLISHING COMPANY (EDINBURGH) LTD
7 Albany Street
Edinburgh EH1 3UG

British Library Cataloguing in Publication Data
Clydesdale Bank
    The Clydesdale collection : paintings from the Clydesdale Bank.
    1. Scottish paintings – *Catalogues, indexes*
    I. Title   II. Bourne, Patrick
    759.2911074

    ISBN 1–85158–312–2

Typeset in 11 on 12 pt Caledonia by Input Typesetting Ltd, London
Printed in Spain

Design and Finished Artwork by James Hutchinson and Paul Keir

Photograph of Sir Eric Yarrow by Graham Lees
Photographs of works of art by Marilyn Muirhead

Many thanks to Lesley Stevens and Fiona MacAulay for all their help in researching
material for this book.

PAINTINGS FROM THE
CLYDESDALE BANK COLLECTION

CONTENTS

PREFACE

The very name Clydesdale Bank conjures up images of the great industries of Scotland, of shipbuilding and heavy engineering, of farming, of whisky, of steel-making and, more recently, of electronics and offshore oil. Throughout its entire history the Bank has been associated with Scotland's industrial and agricultural heartlands and most particularly with the City of Glasgow where it was founded in 1838 and where it still has its head office.

Good banking is not, however, concerned only with monetary values and the harsh realities of success or failure in business and commercial life. It is concerned with people and with those other values which add so much to all our lives. I suspect that it was with this in mind that, when General Manager, my predecessor, the late Sir Robert Fairbairn, set about building the Clydesdale Bank collection of paintings and sculpture.

Here for the first time, in this illustrated volume, is a record of the complete collection. Much of it consists of works by Scottish painters or which feature Scottish subjects and, while most are normally to be found in the Bank's head office, a number are to be seen in offices and branches in Edinburgh, London and elsewhere. No part of the collection is secured in the Bank's vaults as we strongly believe that the paintings should be freely exhibited for the enjoyment of customers and staff.

To mark the recognition of Glasgow as 1990 European City of Culture, the Clydesdale Bank will stage, from July to October, an exhibition of many of its paintings and sculptures in the magnificent Banking Hall at 30 St Vincent Place, itself a work of art. This volume has been planned to coincide with and complement that exhibition and will, I hope, convey to the reader something of the enjoyment and pride with which we in the Bank regard this important part of our Scottish heritage.

I hope that you will be able to visit the exhibition to see these works at first hand and that, on future visits to the Bank's premises, you will watch out for and enjoy other examples from the collection.

Sir Eric Yarrow
Chairman

FOREWORD
THE CLYDESDALE BANK

Whilst to most people the name of the Clydesdale Bank may not readily be associated with fine paintings, anyone who has visited the striking head office in Glasgow, its chief offices in other cities or any of its major branches, will almost certainly have seen, either in the public areas or in the manager's office, evidence of the Bank's collection.

The Bank itself was founded in 1838 but it was not until the 1950s, when it was already some 120 years old, that any significant art purchases took place. The architect of the collection was the late Sir Robert Fairbairn, initially in his capacity as the bank's General Manager and latterly as Chairman. A number of works, mainly portraits, predate Sir Robert's time. Records show that, at the beginning of this century, Sir George Reid and Sir John Lavery were commissioned to paint portraits of two past Chairmen. There is no evidence to suggest, however, that any serious attempt had been made to establish a worthwhile collection prior to that period.

Sir Robert's own taste in art was varied but for the Bank he appears to have favoured Scottish painters and, by extension, Scottish subjects. This continues to be the Bank's policy and additions to the collection have consisted largely of works by living artists. It is also a policy wholly appropriate to the Clydesdale Bank which, over its entire history, has identified closely with the great industries for which Scotland was to become renowned.

The Bank itself is now an integral part of the fabric of Scottish life. It has shared in the lives of countless Scots in their homes, toiling on farms, in shipyards, in steelworks and in every other industrial and business activity from Lerwick to Stranraer and on into England. It has known their successes and disappointments, their triumphs and hardships and has sought always to provide a banking service which understands and is responsive to their needs.

Today, through the Bank's network of 350 branches throughout Scotland, in north-west England and in London, this commitment to service continues. Now a member of the National Australia Bank Group, the Clydesdale Bank has entered a new era, placing even greater emphasis on service and intent on building its business and its reputation until it is recognised as the best Scottish bank in the United Kingdom. Acquired by the National Australia Bank in 1987, the Clydesdale Bank has been revitalised and now has, as sister banks, the Yorkshire Bank in England, the Northern Bank in Northern Ireland and the National Irish Bank in Eire. Abroad it can take advantage of NAB's extensive international presence and, particularly in Europe, it has built up a network of carefully chosen correspondent banks.

THE CLYDESDALE BANK COLLECTION

Since 1987, the Clydesdale Bank has been extensively restructured to improve both its effectiveness and its efficiency and to make it better equipped to succeed in the rapidly changing banking and financial services marketplace. Substantial capital investment has been committed to branch automation and computer systems and intensive training programmes have been introduced to improve the service given to customers by the Bank's 7,000 staff. The Bank's corporate identity, established by Lewis Woudhuysen more than 20 years ago, has also been developed to make it more appropriate for today's needs and to reflect the new association with the National Australia Bank. Taking visual change further, an extensive programme of improvements to branches is underway and a stylish range of corporate clothing has been introduced. By themselves, such visual changes are not important but, as evidence of more fundamental improvements in the Bank's ability to provide better service to customers, they are relevant and present a more fitting image of the new Clydesdale Bank.

All of this is a far cry from that day in April 1838 when the Clydesdale Bank first opened for business in temporary premises at 94 Miller Street, Glasgow. Promoted by a group of businessmen of moderate means, its first Chairman was James Lumsden who is also recognised as the founder of the Bank. Born in 1778 during the American War of Independence, James Lumsden entered the family manufacturing and wholesale business engaged in publishing, stationery and engraving. He served as Lord Provost of Glasgow and it was said of him that 'it is scarcely possible to mention a single local cause or event of a public nature with which he was not intimately connected'. Interestingly, he was also a patron of the arts and provided sponsorship for the artist Horatio McCulloch whose painting, *The Clyde from Dalnottar Hill*, (Plate 40) is one of the major works in the Bank's collection.

Closely linked with some of the great names of the Scottish industrial and commercial scene, men such as John Blackie, Sir Thomas Lipton, Sir William Arrol and Sir Robert McAlpine, the Clydesdale Bank expanded steadily through good times and bad until, in 1920, it affiliated with the Midland Bank. Shortly afterwards, in 1924, another Scottish bank with which the Clydesdale Bank had earlier and unsuccessfully sought a merger – the North of Scotland Bank – also became affiliated to the Midland Bank. As its name suggests, the North of Scotland Bank was particularly strong in the north of the country and was heavily involved in local industries such as farming and fishing. It had its head office in Aberdeen and would make a good match with the Clydesdale Bank, which was strongest in central and south-west Scotland, although merger at that time was still some way off.

Although it was of little significance at the time and probably went completely unnoticed, another interesting fact about the North of Scotland Bank was that it had been the employer of James McBey who subsequently became a well-known and successful artist. He joined as an apprentice in 1899 and, when he left 11 years later to pursue his artistic career, was earning the princely sum of £80 per annum. Three of his paintings *Venice*, *Minsmere* and *In the Artist's Studio* (Plates 37 to 39) are now owned by the Clydesdale Bank.

In January 1950, some 27 years after the merger had been first proposed, the Clydesdale Bank Ltd and the North of Scotland Bank Ltd eventually amalgamated to form the Clydesdale and North of Scotland Bank Ltd, at the time the largest of the Scottish banks. In June 1963 the name was shortened to Clydesdale Bank Ltd. The new bank combined, under the Midland wing, the best features of both the original banks and continued to grow and to build for itself a reputation for being innovative and pioneering. Among its successes were the introduction of cash dispensers, an on-line counter terminal system and electronic funds-transfer at point of sale (EFTPOS).

The Clydesdale Bank, like the other Scottish banks, has retained the right to issue its own banknotes and many beautiful specimens of the engraver's art have been produced over its 152-year history. It is doubtful if any have been more attractive than those available today which feature prominent Scottish historical figures on one side and scenes illustrating their activities on the other. The notes in the current series depict Robert Burns, David Livingstone, Robert the Bruce, Adam Smith and Lord Kelvin.

Just before its 150th anniversary Clydesdale Bank was acquired from Midland Bank by National Australia Bank and took up the role as a member of the NAB Group which it enjoys today. A year later, to mark its anniversary, the Bank published a fascinating history written and researched by Dr Charles Munn. In celebration of its long association with the City of Glasgow the Bank also sponsored the spectacular Clydesdale Bank Anniversary Tower at the highly successful Glasgow Garden Festival. It is fitting, therefore, that a bank so conscious of its Scottish heritage should accept a responsibility to preserve that which is good. It is in this spirit that the Clydesdale Bank Collection has been assembled and we commend to you its paintings and its sculpture.

George Edwards

CHAPTER ONE

The Clydesdale Bank Collection has been formed over the last 40 years; it consists of over 100 paintings and, although there has been no conscious policy beyond acquiring paintings that would give pleasure, dominant themes have evolved – Scottish landscapes, seascapes and country life. The corner-stone pictures by McCulloch, Munnings, Laura Knight, McIntosh Patrick and Alexander Nasmyth all reflect this bias – the Nasmyth is very much of a city set in its landscape – and whilst the paintings are universally uncontroversial and approachable (there is only one abstract, by Alan Reynolds), a number of the works would be worthy of the National Galleries of Scotland.

The works in this collection have been purchased by individuals, not by committee, a policy that has proved successful with other company collections, most notably with that of Robert Fleming and Co. The man most responsible for the Clydesdale Bank Collection was the late Sir Robert Fairbairn. His interests extended beyond Scottish paintings and he added works by Peter Monamy, the 18th-century English seascape painter, and Alfred Munnings, Laura Knight and 'Lamorna' Birch, all of whom worked at Newlyn in Cornwall.

Whilst customers of the Clydesdale Bank have always had access to all the pictures in the collection, the paintings have been scattered around different branches in various cities – Edinburgh, Glasgow, Aberdeen and London. Now that they have all been brought together for this book and for the exhibition in Glasgow this summer, the extent and range of the collection can be appreciated for the first time.

The Clydesdale Bank has a tradition of commissioning leading portrait painters to paint the Chairmen – most notably Sir James King's portrait by Sir George Reid (Plate 62) and Sir James Bell's portrait by Sir John Lavery (Plate 35). These pictures were acquired in 1908 and 1923 respectively, and were the foundation of the Clydesdale Bank Collection. Until the early 1950s, however, they hung on the board-room walls of the Bank with only one another for company, but in 1952 the Bank began making regular additions to the collection, mainly of works by senior, living Scottish artists.

The earliest paintings in the collection are exceptions to this general rule. Peter Monamy's *The Morning Gun* and *The Evening Gun* (Plates 48 and 49) are good examples of 18th-century English shipping paintings – a genre, along with portrait painting, in which English artists excelled at that time. Monamy became famous for his atmospheric depiction of shipping becalmed on placid water and the accuracy of his nautical detail. His paintings have a soft light and a poetic note that indicate a close study and admiration of the earlier Dutch masters. Francis Holman's larger work, *Seapiece with Shipping* (Plate 24), painted perhaps half a century later, is less atmospheric and more of a ship's portrait, although the choppy water is well executed. A firm grasp of the construction and design of such vessels and the detail of rigging are vital elements of this school of painting over which these artists have complete control.

The most important painting in the collection is also the earliest Scottish work. *Edinburgh from Calton Hill, 1825* by Alexander Nasmyth (Plate 56) is the largest of his series of four cityscapes painted in 1824 and 1825. Along with another in the series, *Princes Street with the Royal Institution Building Under Construction, Edinburgh from Calton Hill* was part of the Edinburgh Festival Exhibition 'Painting in Scotland – The Golden Age' in 1986, which was also shown at the Tate in London. In the catalogue, Duncan Macmillan describes them as '. . . of unique importance as urban landscapes . . . the four paintings together constitute a striking record of the city at the height of its fame as the home of the Scottish Enlightenment.' Nasmyth views the city from the base of Calton Hill on the site where William Hamilton's Royal High School was to be built the following year. The rock face on the right of the composition was razed to level the site for the building. Across Regent Road stands the old Calton prison, then the largest prison in Scotland. It was demolished one hundred years later to make way for Thomas Tait's Art Deco St Andrew's House. The view takes in the Old Town to the left and the New Town, nearing completion, to the right. Nasmyth depicts the city as a pleasant, civilised environment, bathed in a mid-summer evening sunlight, with a large number of the city's inhabitants going about their business or merely enjoying the weather. The painting suggests Canaletto in its all-encompassing ambition, and, like the Venetian painter, Nasmyth draws attention to the individuality of each citizen.

Nowadays Alexander Nasmyth is largely associated with landscape painting, due partly to the prolific production of wooded classical landscapes by his family (five daughters and a son were painters). Nevertheless, he was a man of many accomplishments, also designing buildings and bridges, and was a friend of Sir Walter Scott, Robert Burns and Sir David Wilkie. He was concerned with the successful co-existence of the countryside with its inhabitants.

The Clyde from Dalnottar Hill, 1858, (Plate 40) was commissioned by a Greenock shipbuilder, James Tennant Caird, who paid Horatio McCulloch the sum of £420 to paint a scene which McCulloch himself had long admired. In his letter of thanks to Caird, McCulloch wrote: 'I might say a great deal on the subject of the obligation I owe you for giving me an opportunity of painting a scene I had long dreamed of but will content myself with saying I truly thank you . . .'

This celebrated view of the Clyde looking towards Dumbarton, now obscured by the Erskine Bridge and other 20th-century developments, was very popular with Scottish painters during the first half of the 19th century. As well as McCulloch, Alexander Nasmyth, John Knox, John Fleming and 'Grecian' Williams all painted it on more than one occasion. In Lumsden's book *Steamboat Companion* (1831), the view is described as '. . . one of the most admirable prospects perhaps in the world'. McCulloch has treated the composition in a conventional way. A calm reach of the Clyde is framed by trees in the Claudian manner. This is in keeping with the English painter Joseph Farrington's blithely Anglocentric description of the scene as '. . . the most Italian view in England'. The archaic composition, however, stands in imminent threat from the foresters working at the left of the scene. Evidence of their progress through the foreground of the picture is provided by a discarded saw and axe and the trunk and boughs of recently felled trees. In the middle ground a team of horses drag timber towards two working boats waiting on the canal. This interest in the countryside as a working environment has a parallel in the work of Constable, a generation earlier. McCulloch wryly records a classical sylvan setting, enlivened by the cast at work, busily striking the set.

What is so impressive about the painting is the complete success with which McCulloch integrates the rustic detail of the foreground with the magnificent sweep of the landscape beyond. He was the first painter to capture the grandeur of the Scottish landscape, especially the Highlands. Landseer caught the wildness of the mountains in his small, pure landscape panels of the 1830s but McCulloch depicted the beauty of the desolate, remote parts of the North in paintings on a grand scale. Works such as *Glencoe* (1864), in Glasgow Art Gallery, and *Loch Katrine* (1866) are evocations of the Scottish hills that have never been surpassed. Had McCulloch shown more in London (he only exhibited once, at the RA) he would have established a greater and more far-reaching reputation both in his own lifetime and today. However, *The Clyde from Dalnottar Hill* served as a centre-piece in the major exhibition of McCulloch's work staged by Glasgow Musems and Art Galleries in 1988 and is discussed at length in Sheenah Smith's immaculately researched catalogue.

Charles Martin Hardie's *Fishing on a Summer Evening* (Plate 22) an idyllic scene with sand martins swooping to feed over a slow-moving stream and a fisherman changing flies on the far bank, was painted in 1885 and is a good example of a period which is not otherwise represented in the collection.

Louis Bosworth Hurt's *The Hills of Skye* (Plate 30), painted at the turn of the century, is a typical example of this artist's work and it is this subject-matter which has made him popular with Japanese collectors in recent years. Businessmen in Tokyo claim that the contemplation of a Scottish scene by Hurt or Breanski (both Englishmen) makes their Scotch whisky taste even better. Although much of Hurt's work resorts to a formula, he could always be relied on to depict effectively bursts of sunlight on misty hills.

CHAPTER TWO

Sir Alfred Munnings's *The Meet at Mendham* (Plate 55) was acquired by the Bank in 1971 from the celebrated Glasgow dealer Ian McNicol who had known the artist and bought many paintings directly from him over the years.

Like John Constable, Munnings was the son of a Suffolk miller. He painted this picture in 1902 when he was 24 years of age and was living at Shearings Farm near his birthplace at Mendham where he rode with the local hunt. It is painted with complete confidence, made possible by an intimate knowledge of horses and hounds. Although the huntsmens' faces are not drawn in detail, each rider would have been recognisable by his characteristic seat, perfectly caught by Munnings's keen eye. The eager activity of the hounds is captured in a few telling dabs of the brush. The whole scene is painted in an unfussy style and with considerable dexterity. This fluidity is all the more remarkable given that three years previously Munnings had lost an eye in an accident. Half a century later he wrote: 'Even now I often make a stroke in the air which doesn't arrive at the canvas or make another which lands too violently.'

Gypsy Caravans by Dame Laura Knight (Plate 34) was painted in the 1920s and is the product of a fascination with the lives of travelling people that affected many artists in England between the wars. Augustus John, Russell Flint and Alfred Munnings also painted similar subjects and Charles Vyse, the Chelsea potter who designed figures for Doulton, often modelled gypsy figures. These artists identified with the romantic, informal way of life – in particular Alfred Munnings who spent several years travelling around East Anglia in a caravan with a string of horses. Before the war, Laura Knight had lived at the artists' colonies at Staithes in Yorkshire and Newlyn in Cornwall, where she knew Munnings well. In 1918 she and her artist husband, Harold, moved to London and she painted a fresh range of subjects; Diaghalev's Ballet, the theatre, circuses, fairs and gypsy life, for which she became the best-known woman painter in Britain. *Gypsy Caravans* is painted with Laura Knight's customary clarity and strong drawing. The figures are looking away from the painter, the dog in the foreground sleeps. Whilst being intimately close to the subject, the painter is unnoticed and the figures are natural and unposed.

Fisherman on a River (Plate 3), dated 1949, is one of 'Lamorna' Birch's late works. It combines his two passions of painting and fishing in a way comparable to his contemporary, Charles Oppenheimer, the Kirkcudbright artist. Birch had earlier been friendly with Munnings and Laura Knight when they were all living in Cornwall. Unlike them, Birch remained in the West Country for the rest of his life. He took his name, 'Lamorna', from Lamorna Cove where he lived and painted. In later years he made frequent trips to Scotland, especially the Spey Valley, to fish and paint. However, *Fisherman on a River* was probably painted in Devon. He excelled at painting light on water and Laura Knight recalls him spending hours 'watching the effects of sky reflected in the stillish water, ranging from blue and gold-tinged cloud to irridescence'. During the 1920s his landscapes became quite stylised but his later works have an unforced naturalism that is best described as 'late impressionist' and have much in common with George Houston and Charles Oppenheimer. In this picture Birch applies a fisherman's knowledge of river conditions to his recreation of the eddie and swirl of shallow water rounding a bend.

Thomas Cooper Gotch, who painted *Lilies* (Plate 19), was also a Newlyn painter, but exceptional in that he painted symbolist subjects, usually on the theme of youth. Lilies often played a part in these paintings as a symbol of purity and innocence. Here he paints a simple, naturalistic study of the flowers themselves.

The late 19th century witnessed the development of significant schools of avant garde progressive painting outside London. The two most important of these being the Newlyn and Glasgow Schools, the latter represented by work from David Gauld, Sir John Lavery and D. Y. Cameron. The dreamlike atmosphere of David Gauld's *Breton Village* (Plate 16) is in marked contrast to the prosaic sentiment of his later paintings of cattle and calves for which he is now better known. *Breton Village* was painted in Scotland 20 years after he returned from Grez in Brittany. It is deliberately nostalgic in its calculated evocation of fading afternoon light and colour, heightened by the passage of time.

Sir John Lavery's *Princes Street, Edinburgh*, 1921 (Plate 35) shows a former Glasgow Boy's unusual view of Edinburgh. From his choice of vantage, probably a room in the North British Hotel, the dominating presence of Edinburgh Castle is for once reduced. He has made the Scott Monument soar to twice its real height, and this, allied to the adjacent wedges of Princes Street on the one side and the gardens on the other, creates a dynamic of diagonals. The city is washed by the pewter-coloured light of late afternoon and on the horizon Lavery distinguishes the subtle conjunction of cloud and haze perfectly. This is a work of consummate sophistication.

D. Y. Cameron, a fellow Glasgow Boy, painted *Kirkhill* (Plate 5) at the turn of the century. A woman in a bonnet passes serenely through the sunlit village square. In the background three other figures stand motionless and there is a sensation of calm and quiet dignity in keeping with the autumnal hues of the artist's palette. This air of intimacy has been replaced in *Carse of Stirling* (Plate 4) by a feeling of space and distance. The later picture employs a lateral rhythm, punctuated by the twin trees in the foreground and the grouping of haystacks beyond.

James McBey (Plates 37 to 39), the celebrated etcher, was one of the most travelled of Scottish artists. Born in Aberdeen, he spent much of his life in North Africa and several years in the United States. The view of Venice, dated 1925, was the product of the second of two visits there. It is painted with a dash and fluidity similar to the watercolours for which he is better known today. McBey employs bare areas of white canvas to create the illusion of light in the same way he would use the white of watercolour paper, and handles the oil paint with an immediacy more often associated with the freer medium. The collection also includes two typical McBey watercolours, *Minsmere*, which reveals a debt to Rembrandt both in the choice of landscape and in the swift, relaxed exposition of the ink drawing, and *In the Artist's Studio*, a slightly unsettling self-portrait, showing McBey's reflection in a cheval mirror in his well-ordered etching studio.

Charles Oppenheimer painted *Early Morning, Kirkcudbright* (Plate 57) around 1940. Although he spent most of his working life in Kirkcudbright, Oppenheimer was unaffected by the penchant for heavy impasto and flat, decorative colour which many of the Kirdcudbright artists shared with Hornel. Oppenheimer's style reflects a more English sensibility. Originally from Manchester himself, his technique is drier and more literal than the Kirkcudbright School. *Early Morning, Kirkcudbright* is one of many views of the Dee seen from the Stell painted by Oppenheimer. He returned to this scene often, showing the river in various seasons and weather conditions, particularly under snow or in bright sunlight. Remarkable for his consistency, and unaffected by modern trends in Edinburgh or abroad, he painted this work very much as he would have 30 years earlier.

In *Berwick on Tweed, 1900* (Plate 66) Frank Wood presents a similar aspect, looking across a river towards a town. In common with Oppenheimer, Wood fills his painting with precise and detailed observation, but whereas Oppenheimer chooses a time when Kirkcudbright is still and peaceful, Wood positively relishes the bustle and activity of the Berwick quayside.

Cliffs in Orkney (Plate 11) is a study of Stanley Cursiter's native coast. It was painted in 1952 after he had returned to live in Orkney following a distinguished artistic and administrative career spent mainly in Edinburgh. It is painted almost entirely in subdued greys, reminiscent of a Whistler nocturne. Forty years earlier Cursiter had painted a series of futurist-inspired oils that were progressive exercises in the modern movement: for the rest of his career he painted in a much more traditional style. The evocation of the grandeur of the Orcadian cliffs is achieved by sensitive and accurate modulation of tone, similar to the quality found in George Houston's work.

In the Argyll and Ayrshire paintings (Plates 25 to 28), Houston pursues his investigation of landscape and season. The pictures share a similar construction but, in the hands of a patient observer of the countryside, each one creates a precise and specific sense of climatic condition and place. Houston achieves this with a perfect sense of tonal modulation which he also employs in his description of terrain. These landscapes are familiar and calculatedly unspectacular; in their diffidence they become accessible and inviting. In contrast, the five landscapes by Houston's contemporary, Maclauchlan Milne (Plates 44 to 47), possess as much of the character and personality of the painter as they do of the place. They are suffused with a jagged and exotic rhythm, more in keeping with Mediterranean rather than northern mood. Milne shares a sensibility of colour and planar construction with Cadell and Peploe. This is especially apparent in *Corrie, Arran* – the legacy of many years spent painting in Provence.

The only painting in the collection by one of the four Scottish Colourists is Leslie Hunter's *Landscape near Ceres, in Fife* (Plate 31). Although only a minor work, it has a satisfying strength of construction and richness of impasto. On occasion Hunter's spontaneity could produce awkward passages but his work is always redeemed by its innate conviction.

William C. Crawford, of the Crawford's Biscuits family, was free of the financial pressures which feature in the professional lives of most painters. He spent the summer months sailing in the Hebrides but the quality of *Iona* (Plate 6) shows him to be more than merely a talented amateur. Around this time the Hebridean beaches positively thronged with Scottish painters – Peploe, Cadell, John Duncan, Mervyn Glass and Maclauchlan Milne – almost as though a Colourist lurked in every cove. Mary Morris's Iona seascape (Plate 51), painted around the same time, is more conventional in composition than the work of these artists, but she too responds to the startling colours of the shallow waters on a summer's day.

 Cottage Garden (Plate 63) was probably painted at Gatehouse of Fleet in Galloway where Alick Sturrock lived between the wars. It is a good example of his subtly individual way of seeing trees and sunlight. Early in his career he was a member of the Edinburgh Group which included Sir W. O. Hutchison, D. M. Sutherland and Eric Robertson, although he is closer in spirit to the English painter John Nash. Sturrock unites his love and knowledge of plants and trees with a refined, painterly sensitivity to the interplay of light and shade. He explores the various qualities of light – filtered, reflected and direct – all resulting from the contact between natural organic form and aesthetic order that a garden implies. In this seemingly simple painting, Sturrock resolves a set of extremely complex painterly considerations.

 Ploughed Fields, Angus (Plate 59) dates from the late 1940s when McIntosh Patrick's formidable technique was still at the service of an intense pastoral vision. The painting is a celebration of the bucolic ideal. From the vantage of a gently sloping, freshly ploughed field, the artist describes the rhythmic rise and fall of light and shadow playing laterally across the furrows. The shire horses pulling the plough and the fork-hefted haystacks would not be out of place in Samuel Palmer's valley of vision. The countryside beyond, with its mature trees and solid, stone, farm buildings, is the essence of permanence and plenty.

 Painted about 15 years later, *Huntly Burn near Castle Huntly* (Plate 58) demonstrates an increasingly fluid and relaxed technique, but the achievement is over literal and the idiosyncratic spirit is less evident. The painting of the water is flawlessly adroit but implicit in this dexterity is a loss of passion.

CHAPTER THREE

Some of the pictures bought in the early 1950s are typical of the taste of that era and, despite their technical proficiency, seem old-fashioned today. Achibald Kay's three river scenes (Plate 32) give a slightly idealised view of Scotland, as though all painted when the weather and the landscape conspired to be on their best behaviour. Healey Hislop's *Galloway Landscape* (Plate 23) evokes the cosy, rolling aspect of that corner of Scotland, but with less conviction than McIntosh Patrick's Angus landscapes of the same period. James Kay's *Winter, Whistlefield, Loch Long* (Plate 33) is not the artist at his best, due to an overcrowded and confusing composition.

The Edinburgh School is well represented in the collection by work from two past Presidents of the RSA. *Fresh Breezes, St Monans* by Sir William MacTaggart (Plate 41), painted in the late 1930s, shows the early influence in this painter's career of Maurice Vlaminck and Emile Nolde. The steely blues of the sky and sea and the rough, unsettled shoreline, aggressively conjure the sudden bluster of an East coast squall. While the small boats pitch in the harbour, the town and the cliffs of the Isle of May are lit by a watery sun. MacTaggart's vigorous manipulation of the impasto is precisely apt to his subject. *Sunset over Musselburgh* (Plate 42) is a much later work and a typical example of MacTaggart's mature style. The scumbled texture supports a palette dominated by a lurid sun in a boiling sky.

Like MacTaggart, Sir William Gillies worked both in East Lothian and Fife. The little fishing ports along the Fife coast provided him with a rich painting ground in easy reach of Edinburgh. *Old Houses, Anstruther* (Plate 18) has an affinity with Leslie Hunter's Fife pictures and is less idiosyncratic than would be expected from a Gillies watercolour on the same theme.

Adam Bruce Thomson produced his view of *Old Town, Edinburgh, and Arthur's Seat* (Plate 65) around 1940. This is a masterly integration of city and landscape, confronting and resolving the same challenges faced by Alexander Nasmyth a century before. Edifices of tenements and crags resonate together; the flat vertical stone walls of the buildings, angled in the evening light, echo the geological columns of the escarpment behind. Thomson, along with Gillies, Maxwell and MacTaggart, was a member of the Edinburgh School which dominated the RSA exhibitions after the war. Donald Moodie, who painted *Loch Carron* (Plate 50), was also one of their number. During his lifetime he enjoyed a considerable reputation as a teacher and although his paintings are now unfashionable they contain subtleties which should not be overlooked.

Ian Fleming's island landscape, *Shetland Pattern II* (Plate 15) is painted in the style that Fleming had employed for more than 30 years. The tessellated pattern of small fields is finely realised by his planar handling of colour and tone. *Glasgow Tenements* (Plate 14) of 20 years earlier, has the same appreciation of form but with an added attention to texture. The damp, dilapidated stonework and the peeling whitewash appear through an atmosphere heavy with moisture. Amidst this decay the tenements boast a certain bleak grandeur.

Like Ian Fleming, D. M. Sutherland had close associations with the north-east of Scotland – he was born in Wick and was, for many years, head of Grays School of Art in Aberdeen. As a young man he painted many colourful sunlit paintings of the Brittany fishing port of Concarneau. With *Ships from the Faeroes, Aberdeen* (Plate 64), however, he is not attempting to convey any picturesque aspect, but something more fundamental. He shows, in this active, busy picture, the involuntary symbiosis of commerce, bustle, light and grime. The greasy cobbles of Regent Quay and the oiled surface of the harbour water are painted in a narrow range of naturalistic browns and greens. Where the pall of smoke from the railway eddies through the masts of the boats and settles over the city, the paint surface is scumbled and rough.

In stark contrast, Alberto Morrocco's *Winter Sunset*, 1977 (Plate 54) recreates a scene of stillness and purity, infused with a sophisticated humour. Morrocco is best known for his hot, formal, Mediterranean scenes and this painting comes as something of a surprise. Yet even in this snow-covered landscape, as a weak winter sun sets behind the trees, Morrocco suggests a paradoxical warmth and welcome.

Still Life with Fruit, 1952, (Plate 60) is an early Robin Philipson, painted the year he was elected an ARSA. The agitated brushwork demonstrates the influence early in Philipson's career of Oscar Kokoschka and, similarly, the choice of subject and colour owe a debt to Matthew Smith. This painting predates the development of Philipson's unmistakable, idiosyncratic iconography. *The Cardinals* (Plate 61), however, painted more than a quarter of a century later, is a brutal restatement of an obsessive theme. A group of prelates glide and fade in and out of the Stygian half-light, plotting and scheming and seemingly oblivious to the agony of the crucified Christ, towering above them in mute condemnation. The vertical of the cross drives down through the bottom panel of the painting and, transformed in the process from rough-textured wood into a pitch black doorway, it unites the picture in a single, bold gesture.

David Donaldson, generally considered to be one of the most important living Scottish painters, is renowned for his technical and thematic versatility. In *Two Reds* (Plate 13) he eschews the biblical and literary subjects which often feature in his work and concentrates his powers on a relatively humble still-life composition – an earthenware pot, a red capsicum and some fruit.

Alexander Goudie, David Martin, Ernest Hood and John Cunningham have all belonged to the Glasgow Arts Club and the RGI. This coterie can be seen as an alternative bastion of Scottish academic painting, less intellectually biased than the RSA. Most of the recent purchases in the collection have been from this Glasgow-based group. Of these, the best represented is the Lanarkshire-born artist, John Cunningham (Plates 7 to 10). The majority of the 13 Cunninghams are Hebridean coastal landscapes – close cousins to the colourist pictures of 'Bunty' Cadell. Like Cadell, Cunningham is unashamedly *belle peinteur* – these Iona and Colonsay beaches are characterised by a colourist's untroubled enjoyment of paint and intuitive feeling for structure. In particular, *Ross of Mull from Colonsay* (Plate 8), the earliest of the pictures, is as forceful as a Leslie Hunter *Largo* seascape.

Cold Buffet by Goudie (Plate 21) is a deceptively complex composition painted with wit and economy and dependent on a complete control of the artist's personal tonal shorthand. Goudie himself describes this immersion of personality into technique as a journey into a 'magic world where a different language helps explore human experience and makes permanent those transient encounters with the visually stimulating'. Closest in style to the RSA painters is the work of David Martin, especially in *Pansies* and *Flowers in a Glass*, both of which have an affinity with David Maclure's still lifes. *Hills and Farmland, Rhynd* (Plate 43) creates a rhythmic landscape worthy of Gillies.

Consistent with the overall landscape theme of the collection, Mary Armour (Plate 2) is represented by three pastels, of Mull, Connemara and Arran, each of which is characteristic of her landscape work, although she is better known for her still-lifes in oil. From the work of James Morrison, however, two definitive examples are included: *Argyle Street, Glasgow* (Plate 52), a sepia-toned cityscape, and *Strathmore* (Plate 53), an exhilarating Scottish prairie landscape.

John Houston values the medium of watercolour as highly as that of oil – a Scottish tradition that extends back to Arthur Melville. *Evening Sea, North Berwick* (Plate 29) is a Northern Romantic seascape, employing a wet-on-wet technique and deep saturated colour reminiscent of Emile Nolde.

There are also a number of bronzes in the collection by Scottish sculptors. Phyllis Bone is represented by two sensitively modelled works of her favourite subject, horses (Plates 67 and 68), the same subject as Annette Yarrow's powerful *Carthorse* (Plate 69) and Gavin Scobie shows, for him, an unusually academic head of a horse. It has a Hellenic simplicity and a boldness that is reminiscent of Elizabeth Frink. There are also a series of large-scale works by George Wyllie on the theme of banking that display a Jacques Tati-like whimsy allied with a sound and effortless technique.

Scottish painting generally and 20th-century Scottish painting in particular have recently gained an international reputation and following. Each has been discovered by the media and the resulting attention has caused a considerable increase in the prices of some of the better Scottish artists. Whilst it is gratifying that a painting such as McIntosh Patrick's *Ploughed Fields, Angus* has increased perhaps 200-fold in value since it was purchased in 1952, this inevitably means that it will be much more difficult to buy so thriftily in future.

The solution must be to buy against fashion. With the spotlight so focused on the new Glasgow figurative artists, the abstract and semi-abstract painters of the older generation are temporarily being ignored. If the period round the First World War needs to be strengthened in the Clydesdale Bank Collection, then the Edinburgh Group (Sturrock, D. M. Sutherland, Eric Robertson, etc.) as opposed to the fashionable Edinburgh School (Gillies, Redpath, Philipson) has not yet had the attention it deserves. The progress of the Clydesdale Bank Collection over the next few years offers both an opportunity and a challenge. Already an interesting collection with wide appeal it is to be hoped that future additions will maintain and indeed develop the standards set by those whose careful and thoughtful purchases have brought it to this rewarding stage.

PLATES

Plate 1 A. R. W. ALLAN – *A Farm Road*

Plate 2 M. ARMOUR – *Dervaig, Mull*

Plate 3 S. J. 'LAMORNA' BIRCH – *Fisherman on a River*

Plate 4 D. Y. CAMERON – *Carse of Stirling*

Plate 5 D. Y. CAMERON – *Kirkhill*

Plate 6 W. C. CRAWFORD – *Iona*

Plate 7 J. CUNNINGHAM – *Ben More, Mull*

Plate 8 J. CUNNINGHAM – *Ross of Mull from Colonsay*

Plate 9 J. CUNNINGHAM – *Arran from the 'Postage Stamp'*

Plate 10 J. CUNNINGHAM – *Grand Canal, Venice*

Plate 11 S. CURSITER – *Cliffs in Orkney*

Plate 12 D. DONALDSON – *Lustre Jug*

Plate 13 D. DONALDSON – *Two Reds*

Plate 14 I. FLEMING – *Glasgow Tenements*

Plate 15 I. FLEMING – *Shetland Pattern II*

Plate 16 D. GAULD – *Breton Village*

Plate 17 W. A. GIBSON – *Early Summer*

Plate 18 W. G. GILLIES – *Old Houses, Anstruther*

Plate 19 T. C. GOTCH – *Lilies*

Plate 20 A. GOUDIE – *Fishing Boat, Brittany*

Plate 21 A. GOUDIE – *Cold Buffet*

Plate 22 C. M. HARDIE – *Fishing on a Summer Evening*

Plate 23 A. H. HISLOP – *Galloway Landscape*

Plate 24 F. HOLMAN – *Seapiece with Shipping*

Plate 25 G. HOUSTON – *Ayrshire Landscape*

Plate 26 G. HOUSTON – *Ben Cruachan and Loch Awe*

Plate 27 G. HOUSTON – *Loch Fyne*

Plate 28 G. HOUSTON – *Quiet Autumn*

43

Plate 29 **J. HOUSTON** – *Evening Sea, North Berwick*

Plate 30 G. L. HUNTER – *Landscape near Ceres, in Fife*

Plate 31 L. B. HURT – *The Hills of Skye*

Plate 32 A. KAY – *River in Spate*

46

Plate 33 J. KAY – *Winter, Whistlefield, Loch Long*

Plate 34 L. KNIGHT – *Gypsy Caravans*

Plate 35 J. LAVERY – *Sir James Bell*

Plate 36 J. LAVERY – *Princes Street, Edinburgh*

Plate 37 J. McBEY – *Venice*

Plate 38 J. McBEY – *Minsmere*

Plate 39 J. McBEY – *In the Artist's Studio*

Plate 40 H. McCULLOCH
The Clyde from Dalnottar Hill

Plate 41 W. MacTAGGART – *Fresh Breezes, St Monans*

Plate 42 W. MacTAGGART – *Sunset over Musselburgh*

54

Plate 43 D. M. MARTIN – *Hills and Farmland, Rhynd*

Plate 44 J. MacLAUGHLAN MILNE – *Summer Sunshine, Cassis*

Plate 45 J. MacLAUCHLAN MILNE – *Sannox Bay*

Plate 46 J. MacLAUCHLAN MILNE – *Springwell, Corrie, Arran*

Plate 47 J. MacLAUCHLAN MILNE – *Corrie, Arran*

Plate 48 P. MONAMY – *The Morning Gun*

Plate 49 P. MONAMY – *The Evening Gun*

Plate 50 D. MOODIE – *Loch Carron*

Plate 51 M. MORRIS – *Dear Iona, looking to Mull*

Plate 52 J. MORRISON – *Argyle Street, Glasgow*

Plate 53 J. MORRISON – *Strathmore*

Plate 54 A. MORROCCO – *Winter Sunset*

Plate 55 A. J. MUNNINGS – *The Meet at Mendham*

Plate 56 A. NASMYTH – *Edinburgh from Carlton Hill, 1825*

Plate 57 C. OPPENHEIMER – *Early Morning, Kirkcudbright*

Plate 58 J. McINTOSH PATRICK – *Huntly Burn near Castle Huntly*

Plate 59 J. McINTOSH PATRICK – *Ploughed Fields, Angus*

Plate 60 R. PHILIPSON – *Still Life with Fruit*

Plate 61 R. PHILIPSON – *The Cardinals*

69

Plate 62 G. REID – *Sir James King*

Plate 63 A. R. STURROCK – *Cottage Garden*

Plate 64 D. M. SUTHERLAND – *Ships from the Faeroes, Aberdeen*

Plate 65 A. B. THOMSON – *Old Town, Edinburgh, and Arthur's Seat*

Plate 66 F. W. WOOD – *Berwick on Tweed, 1900*

THE ARTISTS

ABBREVIATIONS

A Associate
AC Arts Council of Great Britain
b. Born
CC Corporate Collections, the Fine Art Society (Glasgow) 1990
ECA Edinburgh College of Art
exh. Exhibited
F Fellow
fl. Flourished
GSA Glasgow School of Art
H Honorary Member
IS International Society of Sculptors, Painters and Gravers
NGS National Galleries of Scotland
P President
RA Royal Academy
RCA Royal College of Art
RGI Royal Glasgow Institute of Fine Arts
RP Royal Society of Portrait Painters
RSA Royal Scottish Academy
RSW Royal Scottish Society of Painters in Watercolours
RWS Royal Society of Painters in Watercolours
SAC Scottish Arts Council
SNGMA Scottish National Gallery of Modern Art
SSA Society of Scottish Artists
Tate Tate Gallery, London

ALEXANDER ALLAN RSW
(1914–1972)

Alexander Allan was born in Dundee. He trained at Dundee College of Art, Hospitalfield and in London. In 1968 he was awarded a SAC Travel Award to paint and study in Italy. He was a member of the Glasgow Group and taught at the GSA and also at the Dundee College of Art. Allan was elected an RSW in 1965. He was a portrait painter, landscape painter and draughtsman, and had several exhibitions in Scotland, including a retrospective at Kirkcaldy Art Gallery in 1972. His work can be seen in the collections of the SAC, Glasgow Art Gallery and Graves Art Gallery, Sheffield.

Fig Tree   watercolour   13½ × 20 in.   signed
Spring Landscape   gouache on paper   13½ × 20½ in.   signed and dated 1967

ARCHIBALD RUSSELL WATSON ALLAN RSA
(1878–1959)

Archibald Allan was born in Glasgow and educated there at the Collegiate School and at Greenock Academy. He then attended the GSA, studying under the Glasgow portrait painter, John Spiers. He also studied in Paris, at Julian's and Colarossi's. He was elected to the RSA in 1937. Allan worked mostly in oils and pastels, painting farm and garden scenes, often with animals. His work is represented in several public collections.

A Farm Road   oil on canvas   41 × 48 in.   signed   (Plate 1)

MARY ARMOUR RSA RSW LLD
(b. 1902)

Born at Blantyre in Lanarkshire, Armour studied at the GSA under Forrester Wilson and Greiffenhagen from 1920 to 1925. She taught art in schools in Cambuslang and Glasgow until 1927 when she had to resign following her marriage to fellow artist, William Armour, although from 1951 to 1962 she was on the teaching staff at the GSA. She paints mainly still-lifes and landscapes. Armour was elected an ARSA in 1941 and an RSA in 1958. She is the senior living Scottish woman artist.

Claggan, Connemara   pastel   14 × 18½ in.
Dervaig Mull   pastel   13 × 20 in.   (Plate 2)
Drumadoon Point from Dougrie   pastel   11½ × 21½ in.

SAMUEL JOHN 'LAMORNA' BIRCH RA
(1869–1955)

Samuel John 'Lamorna' Birch was born in 1869 at Egremont in Cheshire, the son of a painter and decorator. At the age of 12 he left school and went to Manchester to work as an office boy, in order to help his mother support the family as his father had died when he was young. Although Birch hated working there, it enabled him to save money to paint and sketch at weekends so as to fulfil his ambition to become an independent artist – an ambition encouraged by his mother. He was soon established as an artist with a promising reputation, selling his work to wealthy industrialists. In 1889, on the strength of the burgeoning reputation of Newlyn as an artists' colony, Birch set off from Cheshire for his first visit to Cornwall, though he did not settle there until 1896. In 1895 Birch, who until then had been entirely self-taught, went to Paris to study at the Atelier Colarossi on the advice of Stanhope Forbes. On his return, he sold every work he had painted there. He then moved permanently down to Cornwall, settling in Lamorna on a farmstead.

The Lamorna Valley provided Birch with an endless variety of subjects to paint, as well as enabling him to pursue the other great love of his life, fishing. He was a prolific painter, exhibiting at the RA from 1893 up to his death in 1955 and sometimes showing as many as six paintings there a year. A frequent traveller, he journeyed throughout England and Scotland in search of good fishing rivers. In 1937 he visited New Zealand and Australia. In 1947 two paintings by Birch were presented to the Queen and Duke of Edinburgh on the occasion of their marriage.

Fishermen on a River   oil on canvas   21½ × 29½ in.   signed and dated 1949   (Plate 3)

LEONARD BODEN
(b. *1911*)

Known mainly as a portrait painter, Boden was born at Greenock and studied at the GSA and Heatherley's. He has exhibited widely, including the RP, RSA and the Paris Salon where he received a gold medal. He has painted official portraits of Queen Elizabeth II, Prince Phillip, Pope Pius XII and other important figures.

The Rt Hon. Lord Maclay   oil   29 × 24 in.   signed

PHYLLIS MARY BONE RSA
(*1896–1972*)

An animal sculptor, Phyllis Bone was born at Hornby in Lancashire. She studied at the ECA and also in Paris and Italy. She lived in Kirkcudbright for much of her working life. Phyllis Bone's work has been exhibited at the RA, the RSA and the RGI. In 1939 she was elected an ARSA and in 1944 was made a full Academician, the first woman to receive the honour.

Carthorse and Snake   bronze   9 in. high   (Plate 68)
Mare and Foal   bronze   11½ in. high   signed and dated 1935   (Plate 69)

EMMET BRADY
(exh. *1896–1928*)

Born in Glasgow, Brady was a marine and coastal painter and etcher. He studied at South Kensington and in Paris. He received a number of awards including the Owen Jones medal, two National silver medals and two bronzes. He was assistant master at the GSA and art master at Kelvinside Academy, Glasgow.

Steam and Sail, Tail of the Bank   oil on canvas   30 × 42 in.   signed

SIR DAVID YOUNG CAMERON RA, RSA, LLD
(*1865–1945*)

A son of the manse, D. Y. Cameron was born in Glasgow in 1865 and educated at Glasgow Academy. He spent a short and somewhat unhappy period in a Glasgow office, studying drawing at the GSA in his spare time. However, in 1885 he decided to concentrate full-time on art, moved to Edinburgh and enrolled at the Royal Institution Schools on The Mound. He exhibited two of his paintings at the RSA as early as 1886, becoming a regular exhibitor at the Academy, the RGI, the RA and the Walker Art Gallery in Liverpool, as well as the Scottish and English watercolour societies. However, it was as an etcher that he first came to prominence. Over a period of some 50 years he etched over 500 plates, becoming one of the foremost British etchers of his day. In his work as both etcher and painter he

Plate 67 P. M. BONE – *Carthorse and Snake*

Plate 68 P. M. BONE – *Mare and Foal*

concentrated on landscape and architectural subjects, excelling in the depiction of the drama and romance of Scottish scenery. He was a superb draughtsman. His work is hung in many public collections both in Britain and abroad. He also had a busy public life, serving for various periods as a trustee of both the NGS and the Tate and as a member of the Royal Fine Art Commission. A stalwart supporter of the Kirk, he did much to stimulate interest in beautifying church interiors. Cameron was knighted in 1924 and, in 1933, he was appointed HM Painter and Limner in Scotland.

Carse of Stirling oil 27½ × 44½ in. signed (Plate 4)
Kirkhill oil 29½ x 45½ in. signed *exh:* CC (Plate 5)

WILLIAM CALDWELL CRAWFORD
(1879–1960)

William Caldwell Crawford was born in Dalkeith and studied at the RSA School and in Paris. He painted mainly landscape and coastal subjects in both watercolour and oil. He was a keen yachtsman and introduced Cadell and Peploe to Iona as he frequently sailed the West Coast and knew it well. Like Cadell he owned a studio in Ainslie Place. Other artist friends included Edwin Alexander and Robert Burns. Crawford was President of the SSA from 1928 to 1930. He was a regular exhibitor at the RSA but declined to become an associate member.

Iona oil on canvas 17 × 23½ in. signed (Plate 6)

JOHN CUNNINGHAM
(b. *1926*)

John Cunningham was born in Lanarkshire in 1926. In the early 1940s he studied at the GSA under David Donaldson, serving in the Scots Guards during the war before returning there to receive his diploma in 1950. From 1967 to 1985 he taught full-time at the GSA. He has travelled regularly to France and Italy, often painting there, and also paints regularly on the west coast of Scotland, particularly at Colonsay and Ardnamurchan. He was elected a member of the RGI and has exhibited there and at the RSA annually. He has also won both the MacFarlane Award and the Cargil Award. His work is in a number of public collections including: the Kelvingrove Gallery, the Hunterian Museum, and the Royal College of Physicians and Surgeons.

Arran from 'The Postage Stamp' oil on canvas 24 × 39 in. (Plate 9)
Barra Seascape oil on canvas 29 × 33½ in. signed
Ben More, Mull oil on canvas 25 × 38½ in. signed (Plate 7)
Boats, La Ciotat oil on canvas 13½ × 23 in. signed
Clearing Sky, Colonsay oil on canvas 25 × 45 in. signed
Colonsay oil on canvas 19½ × 23½ in. signed and dated 1980
Raised Beaches, Colonsay oil on canvas 29 × 36 in. signed
Ross of Mull from Colonsay oil on canvas 28½ × 49½ in. signed (Plate 8)
Seascape, Ardnamurchan oil on canvas 25 × 29½ in.
Silver Tray oil on canvas 29½ × 24 in. signed
The Grand Canal, Venice oil on canvas 19½ × 33½ in. (Plate 10)
The Postage Stamp, Troon oil on canvas 24 × 39 in. signed
Vineyard, Provence oil on canvas 20 × 21½ in. signed

TOM CURR
(fl. *1930–1960*)

Tom Curr was born and brought up in Edinburgh. He exhibited sporadically at the RSA and the RGI during the 1940s and 1950s, his subject matter being horses and farm animals in the West of Scotland. He also executed several portrait commissions including that of William Adamson, Secretary of the Scottish Office.

Ploughing in Glen Clova   oil on canvas   23 × 37 in.   signed

STANLEY CURSITER RSA CBE LLD
(*1887–1976*)

Stanley Cursiter was born in Kirkwall in Orkney and attended the Grammar School there. In 1905 he moved to Edinburgh and was apprenticed as a chromolithographic designer to McLagan & Cummings, Printers. At the same time he studied in the evenings at the ECA where he later became a full-time student, having refused a scholarship to the RCA, London. His holidays were spent in Orkney and it was in Kirkwall that he exhibited for the first time in 1910 and also met Phyllis Hourston who later became his wife. Cursiter kept up to date with the latest artistic developments and, in 1913, inspired by an exhibition of the futurist works shown in London in 1912 and at the SSA in 1913, he painted a series of seven futurist pictures. On his release from war service in France in 1919, Cursiter and his wife travelled to Cassis and Avignon. In 1920 he set up a studio in Edinburgh and, for the next four years, concentrated on large conversation pieces and smaller, more commercial work.

He became a keeper of the NGS and introduced modern conservation techniques, controlling humidity and temperature conditions in the galleries. In 1930 he was appointed Director of the NGS and a member of the RSA in 1937. Cursiter retired from the NGS in 1948 and returned to his native Orkney to devote himself to landscape painting and writing. In the same year he was elected HM Painter and Limner in Scotland and was awarded the CBE. He wrote the standard work on S. J. Peploe in 1947.

Cliffs in Orkney   oil on canvas   27½ × 35½ in.   signed and dated 1952   (Plate 11)

DAVID DONALDSON RSA
(b. *1916*)

Born at Chryston in Lanarkshire, Donaldson studied at the GSA from 1932 to 1937, in 1936 winning the Directors Prize and, a year later, receiving the Haldane Travelling Scholarship which he used to visit Florence and Paris. Upon his return he did an additional year's study at the GSA taking up part-time teaching there from 1938 to 1944. In 1941 he won the Guthrie Award at the RSA. He was appointed a full-time lecturer at the GSA in 1944. He became a member of the RSA in 1962 and Head of the Department of Drawing and Painting in Glasgow in 1967. Donaldson won the Cargil Award in 1969 and received an Hon. LLD from Strathclyde University. He was a founder artist member of the RGI. He has had a number of one-man exhibitions in Glasgow and Edinburgh as well as mixed exhibitions in New York, Canada and France. Donaldson was appointed HM Painter and Limner in Scotland in 1977 and is the leading portrait painter working in Scotland.

Lustre Jug   oil on board   11 × 11½ in.   signed   *exh*: Aitken Dott, 1979   (Plate 12)
Two Reds   oil on canvas   23½ × 23½ in.   signed   *exh*: CC   (Plate 13)

IAN FLEMING RSA RSW
(b. *1906*)

Fleming studied at the GSA between 1924 and 1929. There he met Charles Murray who encouraged him towards engraving and etching, leading him to make printmaking an important element in his art. Now, though he has continued this work, Fleming is primarily known for his oils and watercolours. During the Second World War he served first in the Police War Reserve, recording the Glasgow Blitz on his etching plate. He then joined the army and completed many watercolours of scenes in Europe. From 1931 to 1940 Fleming was a lecturer at the GSA. He then became Warden at Hospitalfield from 1948 to 1954 when he was made Head of Gray's School of Art, remaining there until 1972. At Gray's he introduced printmaking to the curriculum. He founded the Peacock Printmakers and became a friend and associate of William Wilson, whom he regarded as the greatest 20th-century British etcher, through the Society of Artist Printmakers. Together they made many trips to various parts of Scotland and at this time the harbour motif emerged in Fleming's work. Numerous public and private collectors, including the Duke of Edinburgh, own his work. He was elected a member of the RSW in 1946 and a member of the RSA in 1956. He is the Academy's oldest living member.

Glasgow Tenements oil on panel 20 × 27 in. signed *exh*: CC (Plate 14)
Shetland Pattern II 1980 oil on board 29½ × 47½ in. signed (Plate 15)

DAVID GAULD RSA
(1865–1936)

Born in Glasgow, Gauld worked originally as a lithographer before becoming an illustrator on the *Glasgow Weekly Citizen*, and later distinguished himself as a designer of stained glass; his most important commission being the design for the stained-glass windows in St Andrew's Church, Buenos Aires, which took him nearly ten years to complete. Thereafter, Gauld devoted himself entirely to painting. He studied in Paris in 1889 and in 1896 painted at Grez-sur-Loing, a small French village south of Fontainbleau, with a flourishing artists' colony where he painted a series of ethereal landscapes. One of the younger members of the Glasgow School, Gauld was a close friend of Charles Rennie Mackintosh. Gauld's early work was influenced by Rossetti and bridged the gap between the Glasgow School and Art Nouveau before he returned to the more usual Glasgow School style. In his later years he was especially well known for his paintings of cattle and calves. He was elected an ARSA in 1918 and an RSA in 1924. He was made Director of Design Studies at the GSA in 1935.

Breton Village oil on canvas 27½ × 35½ in. signed (Plate 16)

WILLIAM ALFRED GIBSON
(1866–1931)

William Alfred Gibson was born in Glasgow on 19 September 1866 and educated in the city at the National Training College. He gave up a business career to devote his time to landscape painting. Largely self-taught, Gibson was influenced by Corot and the painters of the Hague School. He worked in Scotland, England, Holland and France but lived in Glasgow and was a member of the Glasgow Art Club.

Early Summer oil on canvas 19 × 23 in. signed (Plate 17)

JAMES STIRLING GILLESPIE
(fl. 1950–)

James Stirling Gillespie lives in Torwood, Rothesay. He is a prolific artist mainly in watercolour of west coast subjects.

Arran and St Ninians Bay watercolour 14 × 19 in. signed

THE CLYDESDALE BANK COLLECTION

SIR WILLIAM GEORGE GILLIES RA RSA RSW
(1898–1973)

William Gillies was born in Haddington, East Lothian. His interest in art was encouraged by his uncle, Ryle Smith, an art teacher and watercolourist. He studied at the ECA from 1919 to 1922. The Head of School was David Alison at this time and his assistant, D. M. Sutherland, had a direct influence on Gillies. Adam Bruce Thomson and Donald Moodie were also on the staff, while amongst his fellow students were William MacTaggart and William Geissler. In 1923 he received a travelling scholarship, visiting Italy and France. Gillies returned to Scotland to be appointed art master at Inverness Academy but in 1926 he returned to Edinburgh to take up a part-time post at the ECA where the staff included John Maxwell and fellow student William MacTaggart. During the late 1920s and 1930s Gillies developed a strong and individual watercolour style. Until about 1929 his painting had a formalised, even cubist structure, but later became more free and expressionist. He became a full-time lecturer at the ECA and in 1934 he began to develop a tighter, more linear style in which a pen and ink or pencil outline is set against an expressionist handling of watercolour. In 1946 Gillies became Head of Drawing and Painting at the ECA and a member of the RSA. In 1960 he was made Principal of the College and in 1963 President of the RSW. He was made a CBE, a member of the RA and in 1970 received a knighthood.

Old Houses, Anstruther   oil on canvas   19½ × 24 in.   signed   (Plate 18)

THOMAS COOPER GOTCH
(1854–1931)

Gotch was born in Kettering in Northamptonshire in 1854 and had an extensive schooling in art. He studied at Heatherley's School and the Slade School in London, in Antwerp, and under Jean Paul Laurens in Paris. He moved to Newlyn in Cornwall in 1887 after visiting Australia. He remained in Cornwall for the rest of his life, becoming a central figure in the Newlyn School, although his symbolist subject matter is very different from the realist style of the other members. He exhibited widely, especially in London and on the Continent, and many public collections bought his work.

Lilies   oil on canvas   20 × 16 in.   (Plate 19)

ALEXANDER GOUDIE
(b. 1933)

Alexander Goudie was born in Paisley in 1933 and studied painting at the GSA where he was awarded the Newbery Medal for Distinction. He is a member of the RP and recently did a series of programmes for the BBC called *Portrait* which showed him painting several well-known people: Chris Bonington, Sir Edwin Brammell and Billy Connolly. Goudie is also a member of the RGI who presented him with the Torrance Award. In 1989 a film was made of Goudie painting the flagship of Brittany Ferries and another television programme showed him painting at Goatfell, Arran. He has a French wife and goes regularly to work in her native Brittany, although he lives and works mainly in Glasgow.

Cold Buffet   oil on canvas   41 × 43 in.   signed   *exh*: CC   (Plate 21)
Fishing Boat, Brittany   gouache   20 × 34 in.   signed   (Plate 20)
Portrait of William Thyne   oil on canvas   38½ × 27 in.

LEONARD GRAY

(b. *1925*)

Leonard Gray was born in 1925 in Dundee. He studied at the ECA, completing a post-graduate scholarship there in 1953. His first exhibition was in Edinburgh in 1957 and he was part of the Edinburgh Festival Exhibition at the Crestine Gallery in 1965. He is a member of the RSW, the Aberdeen Artists Society and, in 1972, became a member of the SSA. Leonard Gray's paintings can be found in many public collections including: the RSA Collection, the City of Edinburgh Art Centre, Greenock Art Gallery, Argyll County Council and Dundee Education Authority, as well as many private collections.

East Coast Village   gouache   20 × 34½ in.   signed

BERNARD FINEGAN GRIBBLE

(*1873–1962*)

Bernard Finegan Gribble was born in South Kensington on 10 May 1983. He was the son of the architect, Herbert Gribble, who designed the Brompton Oratory, and first worked under his father before studying drawing at the South Kensington Art Schools under Albert Toft. He exhibited at the RA, the Royal Institute of Painters in Watercolour, the Royal Hibernian Academy and at the Paris Salon, where he received an honourable mention in 1907. From 1912, he was marine painter to the Worshipful Company of Shipwrights.

Corvette   oil on canvas   19½ × 29½ in.   signed

JOHN HALLIDAY

(b. *1933*)

John Halliday was born in 1933 in Kirkcudbright and now works in Edinburgh, making frequent painting trips to other parts of Scotland and the Continent. He studied at the GSA from 1949 to 1953 and won two travelling scholarships from the RSA in 1953, which he used to travel through France and Italy. As well as easel painting, Halliday has done mural work for projects including Prestwick Airport, Scottish and Newcastle Breweries and Culzean Castle for the National Trust. He has exhibited at the RSA and the RGI, and has held one-man shows at the Pelerine Gallery, Paris, in 1968 and at The Great King Street Gallery, Edinburgh, in 1970. His work is in collections thoughout Great Britain, Ireland, France, the United States and Canada.

Ayrshire Landscape   oil on canvas   33½ × 35½ in.   signed
Ben Gairn   oil on canvas   24 × 29½ in.   signed
Evening Bulls   oil on canvas   25 × 30 in.
Near Rullion Green   oil on panel   19 × 19 in.   signed and dated 1982

CHARLES MARTIN HARDIE RSA

(*1858–1916*)

Charles Martin Hardie was born in East Linton and studied at the RSA Life School in Edinburgh. He was an historical and landscape painter, largely in oils but also sometimes using watercolours during his early career, often as studies for the setting of his historical works. He was elected to the RSA in 1895.

Fishing on a Summer Evening   oil on canvas   12 × 16 in.   signed and dated 1885   (Plate 22)

ANDREW HAY
(b. *1944*)

Hay was born in Glasgow and his skills as an artist are largely self-taught. Although he is now based in Cumbernauld his work is still inspired by his native city and recent paintings depicting Glasgow's industrial heritage feature in several public and private collections.

St Vincent Place, Glasgow   oil on canvas   36 × 48 in.

ANDREW HEALEY HISLOP
(*1887–1954*)

Andew Healey Hislop began his studies at the Heriot Watt College. From 1908 to 1913 he attended the ECA where he obtained his diploma in drawing and painting. He was awarded a travelling scholarship and became a student and associate of the British School at Rome. He was in Germany at the outbreak of the First World War and was interned there for four and a half years. In 1918 Hislop was appointed Principal Teacher of Drawing and Design in the printing trades classes at Heriot Watt College. He continued his work there until 1952 when he was made an honorary fellow. Hislop was a prolific artist, painting both in oils and watercolours, he was a fine draughtsman and for ten years did a great deal of etching. He was President of the SSA from 1952 until his death.

Galloway Landscape   oil on board   24½ × 30 in.   signed   (Plate 23)

FRANCIS HOLMAN
(fl. *1767–1790*)

Little is known about Francis Holman. He was of Cornish extraction and lived at Shadwell and at Wapping. Holman had a strong command of atmosphere, a sure knowledge of the shipping trade and was an excellent draughtsman, as seen by the beautifully-drawn small craft in the foreground of his paintings and the meticulous detail of the larger ships. Holman was also particularly adept at portraying the surface of the water, his light feathery touches suggesting movement and transparency. His paintings are in a number of public and private collections including the National Maritime Museum and the Paul Mellon Collection.

Seapiece with Shipping   oil   34¾ × 68 in.   signed and dated 1781   (Plate 24)

GEORGE HOUSTON RSA RSW
(*1869–1947*)

George Houston was born at Dalry in Ayrshire. He trained as a linoleum designer and lithographer in Glasgow before becoming an illustrator on *The Glasgow Evening Citizen* in 1898. Following his work for the paper, Houston took up landscape painting and etching, working mostly in Ayrshire and Argyllshire. His landscapes, done mostly in low-keyed tones, evoke a peaceful contemplative feeling. He exhibited at the RSA from 1898 to 1940 and was made an ARSA in 1909 and an RSA in 1924. In addition, he was also a member of the Royal Institute of Painters in Watercolours from 1920 and belonged to the Society of Twenty-five in London. Houston was a prolific artist partly due to the need to support his family of seven daughters.

Arran from near West Kilbride   oil on canvas   17 × 23 in.   signed
Ayrshire Landscape   oil on canvas   17 × 23 in.   signed   (Plate 25)
Loch Etive   oil on canvas   27½ × 35 in.   signed
Loch Fyne   oil on canvas   17 × 23½ in.   signed   (Plate 27)
Quiet Autumn   oil on canvas   27½ × 35½ in.   signed   (Plate 28)
Ben Cruachan and Loch Awe   oil on canvas   27½ × 35½ in.   signed   *exh:* CC   (Plate 26)

JOHN HOUSTON RSA RSW
(b. *1930*)

Born at Buckhaven in Fife, Houston studied at the ECA, where he has been on the teaching staff since 1955. He was awarded a travelling scholarship in 1953 and travelled to Italy with fellow student, David Michie. He married Elizabeth Blackadder RA in 1956 and they live in Edinburgh, both exhibiting regularly at the Mercury Gallery in London. Houston was elected an ARSA in 1964 and an RSA in 1972. A strong colourist, his work is influenced by Munch and Nolde.

Evening Sea, North Berwick   watercolour   21 × 31 in.   signed   (Plate 29)

GEORGE LESLIE HUNTER
(*1877–1931*)

Hunter was born on 7 August 1877 at Rothesay, Isle of Bute. At the age of 13 he emigrated with his family to California where he helped work on their ranch, but spent all his spare time drawing. It was during this time that Hunter felt he had his best period of training, his self-taught efforts giving him an ability and a gift of perception that no teaching along academic lines could have bestowed. Hunter's parents returned to Scotland in 1898 but Hunter himself chose to stay in California, moving up to San Francisco where he worked as a magazine and newspaper illustrator. In 1906 he was preparing for his first one-man show in San Francisco when the earthquake struck and all his canvases were destroyed. In the same year Hunter returned to Scotland hoping to establish himself as a painter. Initially he was unsuccessful at selling his paintings and was forced to return to his earlier career as an illustrator. He continued painting, however, visiting France a number of times. While in Glasgow his work came to the attention of the dealer, Alexander Reid, who gave him a number of one-man exhibitions, the first being in 1916. Through Reid, Hunter was introduced to a number of people who were to become good friends and life-long patrons. Hunter made an extended visit to the Continent in 1922 and there, in France, he saw a good deal of J. D. Fergusson. From 1924 to 1927 he painted mostly in Scotland, especially Fife and Loch Lomond. In 1927 he moved to the South of France for two years. He had an acclaimed exhibition in New York in 1929 and was part of a very successful group exhibition, 'Les Peintres Ecossais', in Paris in 1931. T. J. Honeyman wrote *Introducing Leslie Hunter* in 1937.

Landscape near Ceres, in Fife   oil on canvas   10 × 14 in.   signed   (Plate 30)

LOUIS BOSWORTH HURT
(*1856–1929*)

Hurt was born and lived in Derbyshire. He studied under the Midlands landscape painter, George Turner. However the majority of his paintings are of the Highlands, usually with cattle, in a style similar to Peter Graham RA. He exhibited mainly in London from 1881 and also in Glasgow.

The Hills of Skye   oil on canvas   24 × 30 in.   signed   (Plate 31)

ARCHIBALD KAY RSA RSW
(*1860–1935*)

Born in Glasgow, Archibald Kay initially pursued a commercial career but, after some years, left to study art in Glasgow under Robert Greenlees. He then went to Paris where he studied at the Academie Julian under Boulanger, Lefèbre and Constant. He exhibited his work at the RA from 1890 and also showed at the Paris Salon and the RSA. He is known for his scenes of Scottish landscapes and rivers. He was President of the Glasgow Art Club and lived in the city for many years.

River in Spate oil on canvas 23½ × 35½ in. signed (Plate 32)
Spring Sunshine oil on canvas 19¾ × 24¼ in. signed
The Rosa Burn, Brodick oil on canvas 27½ × 35½ in. signed

JAMES KAY RSA RSW
(1858–1942)

James Kay was born at Lamlash in Arran. He spent the early part of his life in Glasgow and was in turn a cabinet-making apprentice, bank clerk and insurance clerk, but he always painted in his spare time. He studied at the GSA and his early work was so promising that he gave up ideas of a business career and concentrated on painting. Kay was a fine colourist and his work was in the best tradition of the Scottish School of painting. He was influenced by Turner and Monticelli but developed an individual style, being best known for his paintings on the Clyde. James Kay was a member of the RGI, the Glasgow Art Club and the Union Internationale des Beaux-Arts et des Lettres, France. His first exhibit in the Paris Salon was in 1894 and, five years later, his work was accepted by the RA. He was elected to the RSW in 1897 and, three years before his death, in 1939 was made a member of the RSA. Kay has exhibited at many important art shows in this country, on the continent and in America. His work can be seen in galleries in Bradford, Aberdeen, Stirling, Paisley, Greenock and Auckland, New Zealand.

Winter, Whistlefield, Loch Long oil on canvas 11½ × 17½ in. signed (Plate 33)

DAME LAURA KNIGHT RA
(1877–1972)

Laura Knight was brought up in Long Eaton, Derbyshire, by her mother who encouraged her from an early age to become an artist. She spent a year living with her great-aunt near Paris, returned to England in 1890 and enroled at Nottingham School of Art where she met her future husband, Harold Knight. In 1894 Laura, Harold and Laura's sister, Sissy, went to Staithes in Yorkshire for a month's holiday with her great aunt. After the holiday Laura returned briefly to Nottingham but went back to Staithes the following year and remained there, apart from her visits to Holland, until she went to Newlyn in Cornwall in 1907. Laura and Harold Knight married in 1903 and, for their honeymoon, they went to London, spending much time visiting art galleries, one of which had an exhibition of Dutch paintings, possibly influencing the Knights' decision to visit Holland later. In 1907 the Knights headed for Cornwall where Stanhope Forbes found them lodgings and introduced them to some of his students. It was in Newlyn that Laura began to paint pictures of children on the beach. The First World War brought an end to the Knights' idyllic time in Cornwall and, in 1918, they moved to London permanently. In London Laura found a whole new range of subjects to paint. She began painting Diaghalev's ballet and the theatre in the 1920s and moved on to the circus and gypsies over the years that followed. She was made an ARA in 1927 and a Dame of the British Empire in 1929, becoming a full Academician in 1936. In the same year she also wrote her autobiography *Oil Paint and Grease Paint*.

Gypsy Caravans oil on canvas 19 × 29½ in. signed (Plate 34)

SIR JOHN LAVERY RA RSA
(1856–1941)

Born in Belfast, Lavery was orphaned at an early age and brought up by relatives in Ulster and later Ayrshire. He studied at the GSA, at Heatherley's in London, the Atelier Julian in Paris under Bougereau and at the Atelier Colarossi. In Paris he was influenced by the work of Bastien-Lepage and, along with a number of other young artists, went to Grez-sur-Loing where he painted *en plein air*. In 1885 Lavery returned to Glasgow and began exhibiting at the RSA. In the same year he also completed his first major work, *The Tennis Party*, which was shown at the RA in 1886 and in Munich in 1890, where it did much to enhance the international reputation of the Glasgow Boys, of which Lavery was a leading member. At the Glasgow Exhibition of 1888, Lavery was commissioned to paint the official picture of Queen Victoria's visit. This brought him many more commissions and assured his reputation in international society as a portrait painter. Lavery travelled to Morocco in 1890 and returned there several times, finally establishing a winter retreat at Tangier. He moved permanently to London in 1896 where he associated with Whistler, founding the International Society of Sculptors, Painters and Gravers with him in 1898. He was elected an ARSA in 1892, an RSA in 1896, an ARA in 1911 and an RA in 1921; he was knighted in 1918. He died at Kilmaganny, County Kilkenny, on 10 January 1941.

Princes Street, Edinburgh   oil on canvas   29 × 23 in.   signed and dated 1921 on reverse   *exh*: CC   (Plate 36)
Portrait of Sir James Bell   oil on canvas   57 × 40 in.   signed   (Plate 35)

JAMES McBEY
(1883–1959)

James McBey was born at Newburgh in Aberdeenshire on 23 December 1883. In 1889 he joined the North of Scotland Bank in Aberdeen and during that time he attended evening classes at Gray's School of Art in Aberdeen, as well as private art lessons. In 1910, McBey resigned from the bank to concentrate on his art. He moved to London and held his first exhibition of etchings in 1911 at Goupils which was a great success. Thereafter McBey gained a considerable reputation as an etcher and a watercolourist. In 1917 he was appointed Official War Artist to the Egyptian Expeditionary Force and accompanied the advance through Palestine and Syria. He travelled extensively throughout his life, visiting Holland, France, Spain and Morocco. At the outbreak of the Second World War he was in the USA and stayed there until 1946, taking US citizenship in 1942. During the latter part of his life he lived in Tangier where he continued to paint until his death in 1959. In memory of her husband, McBey's widow donated a sum of money which was used to create the McBey Library and Print Room at Aberdeen Art Gallery.

In the Artist's Studio   watercolour   11½ × 16½ in.   signed and dated 1914   (Plate 39)
Minsmere   watercolour   5½ × 12 in.   signed, inscribed and dated 1919   (Plate 38)
Venice   oil on board   21 × 36½ in.   signed, inscribed and dated 1925   *exh*: CC   (Plate 37)

HORATIO McCULLOCH RSA
(1805–1867)

Horatio McCulloch, regarded as one of Scotland's finest Victorian painters, was born in Glasgow, the son of Alexander McCulloch, a textile manufacturer. It was not easy for a young artist in Glasgow at that time. There was no publicly-funded art school, no strong tradition of patronage and no regular exhibitions of modern art until 1828. McCulloch studied under the Glasgow landscape painter, John Knox, whose reputation was made by his panoramic views of Scotland. Another young artist who studied with Knox at the time was Daniel McNee who became a distinguished portrait painter and McCulloch's lifelong friend. Although there were no regular exhibitions on view McCulloch had other opportunities for study. The old Theatre Royal had a collection of scenery by Alexander Nasmyth and David Roberts. The broad effects of the latter artist's work allowed McCulloch to draw contrasts with the detailed techniques of Nasmyth and Knox. In 1824 McCulloch left home and got a job, first as a snuff-box decorator with Messrs Smith at Cumnock, Ayrshire, and then with William Home Lizars, the Edinburgh engraver. In September 1828 the first 'West of Scotland exhibition of the works of living artists' opened in Glasgow's recently completed Argyll Arcade under the patronage of the Glasgow Dilettanti Society. McCulloch was represented by four works. Public opinion towards his work was at this time rather mixed, his presentation of sketches was not usual practice and many people found his fluid style, which discarded elaborate finish, as somewhat wanting. He had been influenced in this direction by the work of the Revd John Thomson of Duddingston and also by his own direct observations of nature.

McCulloch was lucky to find in James Lumsden his first generous benefactor, for his painting was not bringing him a steady enough income. To supplement it he continued to do decorative work: landscape panels for steamship interiors, patriotic transparencies and scene painting for provincial theatres. He shared the task of providing illustrations for Lumsden's guidebook, *Steamboat Companion*, and was then employed as an illustrator for William Beattie's *Scotland*. On this commission he worked alongside the well-established topographical artists, Thomas Allom and W. H. Bartlett. In 1932 the Dilettanti Society held its exhibition in the new rooms at Buchanan Street and McCulloch was made a committee member. He exhibited regularly with the Scottish Acadamy (later the RSA) and was elected an associate in 1834. In 1835 he moved to Hamilton. Cadzow Forest was now on his doorstep as well as other favourite painting subjects such as Bothwell Castle and the Clyde Valley. However, though he found several patrons in this period, he missed his friends and the lack of an artistic community and was glad to move to Edinburgh in 1838. In this year he was made a full member of the Scottish Acadamy.

McCulloch flourished after the move to Edinburgh. In 1841, annual exhibitions of modern art resumed in Glasgow, organised by the recently formed West of Scotland Academy, and McCulloch's work was on show and received mixed praise. In 1843 his work was hung at the RA for the first and only time. In the 1840s he painted some townscapes moving away from his usual Highland views. McCulloch's work can be seen in many public collections including: the NGS, Glasgow Art Gallery and Museum, Perth and Dundee Art Galleries as well as being part of many private collections in Scotland.

The Clyde from Dalnottar Hill, 1858   oil on canvas   43 × 71 in.   exh: RSA, 1859 No 162 (lent by James Tennant Caird who commissioned the painting)   Glasgow International Exhibition, 1888   CC   (Plate 40)

GEORGE MACKIE RSW
(b. *1920*)

Born at Cupar in Fife, Mackie studied at Dundee College of Art for three years before the war and at Edinburgh and abroad for three years after the war. He is a member of the RSW and the SSA. He is also a Fellow of the Society of Industrial Artists. Mackie has exhibited consistently at the RSA and at the Aberdeen Artists Society over the years. His work can be found in various public collections including the SAC, the University of Edinburgh and Aberdeen Art Gallery.

Blue Boat, Blue Clouds   watercolour   9 × 12½ in.   signed, inscribed and dated 1967

WILLIAM DOUGLAS McLEOD
(*1892–?*)

Born at Clarkston in Renfrewshire, McLeod worked in a bank from 1906 to 1915 and then did war service in the Royal Artillery. He took up art and studied at the GSA from 1919 to 1923. He was a cartoonist for the *Glasgow Evening News* from 1920 to 1930. A landscape painter in oils and pastels, McLeod was also known as an etcher and painted views in Algeria, Spain, Italy and Belgium amongst other places. He exhibited at the RSA, the RGI and the Paris Salon.

Highland View   oil on canvas   28 × 36 in.   signed and dated 1948

SIR WILLIAM MacTAGGART PRSA RA
(1903–1981)

MacTaggart was born at Loanhead, on the outskirts of Edinburgh, the grandson of William MacTaggart, RSA. He studied part-time at the ECA from 1918 and made the first of a number of annual trips to the South of France in 1923, had his first one-man show in Cannes in 1924 when he was 21 and, in the same year, met Matthew Smith at Cassis. MacTaggart first sent work to the RSA in 1921 and was a founder member of the 1922 Group. He joined the Society of Eight in 1927 and, in 1929, had his first one-man show in Scotland at Aitken Dott, Edinburgh. MacTaggart was influenced primarily by Rouault and Munch; he had seen Munch's work at an exhibition in 1931 at the SSA. He was elected President of the SSA in 1933 and, in the same year, began to teach part-time at the ECA, which he continued to do until 1956. During the Second World War MacTaggart was honorary exhibition organiser of the Council for the Encouragement of Music and the Arts. After the war he resumed his trips to France. He was elected an ARSA in 1937 and an RSA in 1948, serving as Secretary of the Academy from 1955 to 1959 and President from 1959 to 1969. He was knighted in 1962, was elected an ARA in 1968 and an RA in 1973.

Fresh Breezes, St Monans   oil on canvas   27½ × 35½ in.   signed   (Plate 41)
Sunset over Musselburgh   oil on board   27 × 36 in.   signed   (Plate 42)

DAVID M. MARTIN RSW
(b. 1922)

Born in Glasgow, Martin studied at the GSA until the Second World War intervened. He then served for four years in the RAF, mostly in India, resuming his studies afterwards and finally completing them in 1948. After a further year at Jordanhill Teachers' Training College, Martin commenced teaching in 1949 and had a successful career as a teacher before retiring early in 1983 in order to paint full-time. He was elected a member of the SSA in 1949, the RSW in 1961 and the RGI in 1981. Martin shows regularly at these societies' annual exhibitions and has taken part in many other group exhibitions. He has been the recipient of numerous prizes and awards including the Robert Colquhoun Memorial Art Prize and the May Marshall Brown Prize. His works are in many public and private collections including the AC and the City of Edinburgh Art Collection.

Flowers in a Glass   oil on canvas   24 × 14 in.   signed
Hills and Farmland, Rhynd   oil on canvas   19 × 23 in.   signed   (Plate 43)
Lilies in the Village, Eaglesham   watercolour   29 × 22¼ in.   signed
Pansies   oil on canvas   19 × 14½ in.   signed

JOHN MacLAUCHLAN MILNE RSA
(1886–1957)

John Maclauchlan Milne was born in Edinburgh and came from a family of well-known Scottish landscape painters. Both his father, William Watt Milne, and his uncle, Joseph Milne, painted naturalistic coastal scenes after the fashion of the Hague School. Before the First World War John lived at Kingoodie near Dundee and he too painted Fife and Tayside scenes in the Dutch idiom. During the war, he served in the Royal Flying Corps and afterwards returned briefly to Dundee but, by the end of 1920, Milne was working in Paris painting a series of street scenes. Shortly afterwards he set out for the South of France which had already been colonised by the likes of Cezanne, Van Gogh and the Fauves. The advances Milne had made in Paris were consolidated on the Rivièra. The light and radiance of the sun accentuated colour to a strong degree, an effect Milne found highly satisfactory, so much so that thereafter he began to spend much of the year in France. Milne often stayed at Cassis where he met Cadell, Peploe and Duncan Grant whose company enhanced his own development. He made trips to the Scottish Highlands where he applied his French attitudes to the Scottish landscape. At the outbreak of the Second World War and the break up of his marriage, Milne came back to Scotland permanently and settled on Arran. He was made an RSA in 1937.

Corrie, Arran   oil on canvas   27½ × 35½ in.   signed   (Plate 47)
Sannox Bay   oil on board   19 × 23 in.   signed   (Plate 45)
Springwell, Corrie, Arran   oil on canvas   19½ × 24 in.   signed   (Plate 46)
Summer Sunshine, Cassis   oil on canvas   19 × 23 in.   *exh*: CC   (Plate 44)

PETER MONAMY
(c. *1686–1749*)

Peter Monamy is an important figure in the history of marine painting in England as he, with Samuel Scott, John Cleveley the Elder and Brooking, helped lay the foundations of the English marine school. In spite of this distinction, little is known about Monamy. He was born in Jersey and came to London at an early age becoming a house painter. By studying the van de Veldes and by constant practice Monamy began to establish a reputation as a marine painter and was highly esteemed by members of the seafaring community. Monamy's oil paintings are well known for their good colouring and accurate rendering of ships and small craft; he was best at portraying peaceful scenes showing ships at anchor. Thomas Hogarth painted a picture entitled *Monamy Showing a Picture to Mr Walker* in which Monamy is displaying his work to Thomas Walker, commissioner of customs and a noted collector of Dutch and Italian pictures. A number of Monamy's oil paintings are in the National Maritime Museum. In addition, the British Museum has some of his pen and wash drawings.

The Evening Gun   oil on canvas   27 × 43½ in.   (Plate 49)
The Morning Gun   oil on canvas   24½ × 29 in.   (Plate 48)

DONALD MOODIE RSA
(*1892–1963*)

Donald Moodie was born on 24 March 1892. He was educated at George Heriot's School and then served in the Royal Scots during the First World War. From 1919 to 1955 he taught at the ECA, where he was influential as a teacher of drawing, being an excellent draughtsman himself. He received the Guthrie Award from the RSA, becoming an Academician in 1952, and was President of the SSA from 1937 to 1942. Moodie was one of an important group of Edinburgh artists, including Gillies and Maxwell, who created a significant episode in Scottish art from the 1930s onwards. He painted landscape extensively, Wester Ross, Ardnamurchan and Brittany being favourite subjects. His work can be found in many public and private collections.

Loch Carron   oil on canvas   19 × 29½ in.   signed   (Plate 50)

MARY MORRIS
(fl. c. *1920–1950*)

Mary Morris was principally a painter of landscapes. She lived at Pollockshields and later moved to Saltcoats. She exhibited at the RGI in 1944 and her work is represented in Glasgow Art Gallery.

Dear Iona, looking to Mull   oil   21 × 31 in.   signed   (Plate 51)

JAMES MORRISON ARSA RWS
(b. *1932*)

Born in Glasgow in 1932, Morrison studied at the GSA from 1950 to 1954 and then taught there part-time until 1958. In 1957 he was elected a member of the SSA and a year later the RGI awarded him the Torrance Memorial Prize. The same year he became a founder member of the Glasgow Group and moved to Catterline, Kincardineshine. In 1959 he was elected a member of the RGI and from 1964 to 1967 Morrison was a Council Member of the SSA. In 1965 he moved to Montrose and joined the staff of Duncan of Jordanstone College of Art, Dundee, where he remained until 1987 having become Head of Department in 1979. He was elected a member of the RSW in 1970 and became an ARSA three years later. Morrison has also had some involvement with the media. He was presenter on the BBC Arts programme *Scope* from 1968 to 1971 and recently, in 1988, was writer and presenter of the STV series *The Scottish Picture Show*. Over the years he has taken several painting trips abroad; he won an AC Travelling Scholarship to Greece and, from 1976 to 1985, painted in various regions of France, taking an extended trip to Canada in 1987. He has had numerous exhibitions in Britain and has also shown his work in Europe and Canada.

Argyle Street, Glasgow   oil on canvas   42 × 41½ in.   signed and dated 1959   *exh*: CC   (Plate 52)
Strathmore   oil on board   30½ × 58½ in.   signed   (Plate 53)

ALBERTO MORROCCO RSA RSW
(b. *1917*)

Alberto Morrocco was born in 1917 of Italian parents. He studied at Gray's School of Art under James Cowie and Robert Sivell from 1932 to 1938. The following year was the first of his many study trips, this time to France and Switzerland. Since then Morrocco has done much travelling, particularly in his native Italy, where he derives inspiration for some of his paintings. From 1940 to 1946 he served in the army; the RSA presented him with the Guthrie Award in 1942. In 1950 Morrocco was appointed Head of Painting at Duncan of Jordanstone College of Art, Dundee, and he continued to teach there until 1982. He was made a member of the RSA in 1962 and three years later was elected a member of the RSW. The RP made him a member in 1975 and so did the RGI in 1979. Morrocco has exhibited regularly since 1949. He has undertaken important portrait commissions including HM the Queen Mother, the President of Iceland and the Earl of Mar and Kellie. His work is in numerous public collections including the SNGMA and the RSA.

Winter Sunset   oil on board   25½ × 28½ in.   signed and dated 1977   (Plate 54)

SIR ALFRED JAMES MUNNINGS PRA RWS
(*1878–1959*)

Born on 8 October 1878 at Mendham in Suffolk, Munnings left school at 14 and was apprenticed to a firm of lithographic printers in Norwich where he was trained in the technique of poster design and printmaking. Munnings remained with the firm of Page Bros & Co. for six years during which time he attended evening classes at Norwich School of Art, all the while gaining a strong reputation in the field of poster design. It was through his job there that Munnings met his first patron, John Shaw Tompkins, director of Caley's Chocolates. On leaving Page Bros in 1898, Munnings returned to Mendham where he lived at Shearings Farm until 1903, buying a studio nearby to concentrate on his paintings. There he established his reputation as a painter of equestrian subjects, producing a number of paintings of country life, horse fairs, hunt scenes and race meetings. He first exhibited at the RA in 1898 but continued to do a bit of commercial work and, in 1899, won the Gold Medal at the Poster Academy at Crystal Palace. In the same year, following an accident, Munnings lost the sight in his right eye. From 1908 to 1916 he spent time painting in Newlyn, Cornwall, where he came into contact with a number of other artists including Laura Knight and Stanhope Forbes. His first one-man show was held at the Leicester Galleries in 1913. During the last two years of the First World War, Munnings was attached to the Canadian Cavalry Brigade as Official War Artist in France. From 1918 he lived at Dedham in Essex. He was elected an ARA in 1919, an ARWS in 1921, an RA in 1925 and an RWS in 1929. From 1944 Munnings was President of the RA but resigned his position in 1949 following his controversial condemnation of modern art.

The Meet at Mendham   oil on canvas   18¼ × 27 in.   signed and dated 1902   (Plate 55)

ALEXANDER NASMYTH
(1758–1840)

Born in Edinburgh, Nasmyth was the son of a master builder who had a share in the building of George Square in Edinburgh. Nasmyth took an interest in building and engineering from an early age which he never lost. He was educated at the Royal High School before being apprenticed to a coach-painter, attending the Trustees' Academy in Edinburgh under the direction of Alexander Runciman. In 1774 he was discovered by Allan Ramsay who took him to London as his assistant. Here he worked for four years, learning at the hand of an established master and studying Ramsay's collection of Old Master paintings and drawings, including landscapes by Claude and Ruisdael. On his return to Edinburgh in 1778 Nasmyth began to paint portraits and family groups. One of his first patrons, Patrick Miller, financed Nasmyth's visit to Italy in 1782. There he became very keen on landscape painting, being particularly influenced by Claude Lorrain, and stated his ambition to turn from portraiture to landscapes. On his return to Scotland in 1785 Nasmyth made the aquaintance of the poet, Robert Burns, and the two began a longstanding friendship.

In the late 1780s or early 1790s Nasmyth opened a drawing school where he taught landscape painting and, as they came of age, each of his seven daughters was trained to take over the teaching of his classes under his superintendence. Nasmyth was involved in the picturesque movement in Scotland at this time, helping to shape the actual landscape to bring it into accord with classical ideals. To this end he designed and built classical temples, installed bridges and ruins and helped his patrons to select suitably picturesque sites for their estates. Nasmyth favoured views of open vistas, often regarded as looking very Italian. He also painted views of Edinburgh, either sweeping panoramas or narrower aspects of the city's architectural features. Nasmyth had a very classical approach to landscape painting but also, through the influence of his son, Patrick, had a feel for 19th-century romanticism.

Edinburgh from Calton Hill, 1825   oil on canvas   47½ × 65 in.   signed   *exh*: CC   (Plate 56)

CHARLES OPPENHEIMER RSA RSW
(1875–1961)

Charles Oppenheimer was born in Manchester, studying at the Manchester School of Art under Walter Crane and also in Italy. He exhibited at the RA, RSA, in the provinces and widely abroad. He lived in Kirkcudbright for many years, painting in both oils and watercolours. His landscapes are accomplished and his watercolour technique sophisticated, being fresh, direct and realistic. A keen fisherman, Oppenheimer captures the effects of light on moving water or snow with great success. He was elected a member of the RSW in 1912 and in 1934 to the RSA. He is represented in many public and private collections, and was one of the artists portrayed by Dorothy L. Sayers in *Five Red Herrings*.

Early Morning, Kirkcudbright   oil on canvas   30 × 40 in.   signed   (Plate 57)

JAMES McINTOSH PATRICK RSA
(b. 1907)

Born in Dundee, the son of an architect, James McIntosh Patrick enrolled at the GSA in 1924 where he studied under Greiffenhagen. There he won a number of prizes and received a Post-Diploma scholarship. On the merits of his early talent as an etcher, McIntosh Patrick received a commission from a London dealer for editions of prints in 1927. However, with the collapse of the market during the Depression McIntosh Patrick diversified into watercolours and oils and in 1930 took a part-time post at the Dundee College of Art where he made illustrations for postcards and journals. McIntosh Patrick began exhibiting at the RSA in 1926 and showed at the RA from 1928. His work was well received from the outset, with pictures acquired for many public galleries, including an oil bought by the Tate in 1935. McIntosh Patrick painted some portraits but is best known for his realistic, detailed landscapes, generally of an agricultural nature. His subjects are mostly taken from the Angus landscape around Dundee, where he still lives and works.

Huntly Burn, near Castle Huntly   oil on canvas   30 × 24 in.   signed   (Plate 58)
Ploughed Fields, Angus   oil on canvas   29 × 39½ in.   signed   *exh*: CC   (Plate 59)

SIR ROBIN PHILIPSON PPRSA HRA RSW
(b. 1916)

Robin Philipson was born in 1916 at Broughton-in-Furness and educated at Dumfries Academy. He studied at the ECA from 1936 to 1949 and, after serving in India in the King's Own Scottish Borderers from 1940 to 1946, joined the staff at the ECA in 1947. In 1948 Philipson was elected a member of the SSA and, in 1951, he received the Guthrie Award from the RSA who made him an Associate the following year. He was made a member of the RSW in 1955 and became Head of the School of Drawing and Painting at the ECA in 1960. In 1960 he became an RSA and three years later a Fellow of the Royal Society of Arts. He was made President of the RSA in 1973 and was knighted for service to the Arts in Scotland in 1976. He was made a member of the RA in 1981. Philipson has exhibited extensively, in particular at the Scottish Gallery in Edinburgh and Roland Browse and Delbanco in London. His work is in many public and private collections including: the SNGMA, the RSA and the British Council.

Still Life with Fruit   oil on canvas   13½ × 18½ in.   signed and dated 1952   *exh*: CC   (Plate 60)
The Cardinals   oil on board   38½ × 46½ in.   signed and dated 1979   (Plate 61)

DAVID POOLE
(fl. 1950–)

David Poole lives in Surrey and has exhibited regularly at the RA from the 1950s onwards. He is the current President of the RP.

Portrait of Sir Robert Fairbairn   oil on canvas   36 × 27 in.   signed and dated 1979

SIR GEORGE REID PRSA HRSW
(1841–1913)

Born in Aberdeen, Reid served as an apprentice to a lithographic firm there before going to Edinburgh to study at the Trustees' Academy in 1862. On seeing a picture by the Dutch artist, G. A. Mollinger, Reid was so impressed that he wrote to the artist requesting whether he would receive him as a student. Mollinger agreed and Reid went to Utrecht for a long stay where he became a close friend of Josef Israels and other Hague School painters. Reid also spent a year in Paris, studying under Adolphe Yvon at the

Ecole des Beaux Arts. In 1869 Reid returned to Aberdeen where he became a successful painter of portraits, especially of men, which were known for their vividness and simplicity. Reid also painted some landscapes, showing a preference for subdued colour, similar to the contemporary Dutch painters of the time. From the late 1870s Reid painted some flower pieces, again using colour sparingly. He was elected an ARSA in 1870, an RSA in 1877 and was named President of the RSA in 1891, the same year in which he was knighted. In 1902 Reid retired his presidency to concentrate on portraiture.

Portrait of Sir James King Bart, LLD   oil on canvas   44 × 29 in.   signed with monogram   (Plate 62)

ALAN MUNRO REYNOLDS
(b. *1926*)

Alan Reynolds was born on 27 April 1926 at Newmarket in Suffolk. He left elementary school at 14, and began drawing and painting at the same time, painting without tuition until the age of 21. However, after the war, which he spent with the Suffolk Regiment and the Highland Light Infantry in France, Belgium, Holland and Germany, Reynolds attended two courses for teachers' training and art and was given a job as an educational sergeant in Germany. During this time he saw an exhibition of works by painters of the Blue Rider group and became influenced by the paintings and writings of Paul Klee. In 1947 Reynolds returned to England and became a full-time student at the Woolwich Polytechnic School of Art. He studied there until 1952, when he was awarded a scholarship to the RCA. From his early interest in landscape, Reynolds' style has unfolded in stages towards abstraction. Throughout his work runs a basic theme of equilibrium and balance. Form and colours (mostly of an earthen range) are used in a dynamic way to express their interrelation, with the ultimate aim of expressing balance.

Composition with Blue Ovoid   tapestry project, oil on board   19½ × 20 in.

JAMES D. ROBERTSON RSA RSW
(b. *1931*)

Born in 1931 at Cowdenbeath in Fife, Robertson studied at the GSA from 1950 to 1956. Following his studies he taught first at the Keith Grammar School in Banffshire, and in 1959 became a part-time lecturer at the GSA. He had his first exhibition in Edinburgh in 1961, since when he has had numerous one-man exhibitions in Scotland and London and has participated in group exhibitions in both Great Britian and the USA. Robertson was elected a member of the RSW in 1962, ARSA in 1974, the RGI in 1980 and the RSA in 1989. At present he is Senior Lecturer in the Department of Drawing and Painting at the GSA.

Incident in a Landscape   oil on canvas   21 × 17 in.   signed

GAVIN SCOBIE
(b. *1940*)

Born in Edinburgh, Scobie studied painting at the ECA from 1958 to 1962. He did not take up sculpture until 1966 and has been a full-time sculptor since 1974. He was given a touring one-man show by the SAC in 1974 and at Inverness Art Gallery in 1977. Since 1983 most of his sculpture has been in terracotta. On the whole his work has been uncompromisingly modern and he was represented by an abstract work in the National Gallery of Modern Art's exhibition 'Scottish Art Since 1900' in 1989.

Book   bronze   17 in. high
Horse's Head   bronze   12½ in. high

THE CLYDESDALE BANK COLLECTION

ALICK RIDELL STURROCK RSA
(1885–1953)

Born in Edinburgh, Sturrock started his career by serving as an apprentice with a firm of lithographers. He studied at the ESA and the RSA Life Class. He also attended the RGI where he met Eric Robertson and D. M. Sutherland with whom he became life-long friends. Together they formed the Edinburgh Group, some of whose influential members included W. O. Hutchinson, John R. Barclay and Spence Smith. He painted mainly in oils, often applying paint thinly and rarely including figures or animals in his pictures. His style of landscape painting developed and reached maturity during his frequent visits to Dorset where he found the English countryside much to his liking. During that period much of Sturrock's work dealt with rural subjects: farm buildings, haystacks, ponds and huge trees. He was elected an RSA in 1937 and became Treasurer of the Academy the following year. Sturrock was married to the artist Mary Newbery.

Cottage Garden   oil on canvas   24 × 29 in.   signed   (Plate 63)

DAVID MacBETH SUTHERLAND RSA
(1883–1973)

D. M. Sutherland was born at Wick, Caithness. He studied at the RGI and Edinburgh and attended the RSA Life Class from 1906 to 1909 under the tutelage of Charles Mackie who greatly influenced him. He was the first recipient of the Carnegie Travelling Scholarship which he used to paint in Spain and Paris in 1911. Most of his summers from 1920 to 1924 were spent in Concarneau, Brittany, where much of his best work was done. In 1927 he and his wife Dorothy Johnstone moved to Joppa, and the summers of 1927 to 1930 were spent painting in Caithness. In 1935 and 1937, and frequently after the war, he was in Plockton, Ross-shire, with Gillies and Adam Bruce Thomson. He moved to Cults, Aberdeenshire, in 1939 and lived there for the rest of his life. In 1936 Sutherland became a member of the RSA and Head of Gray's School of Art, Aberdeen.

Ships from the Faeroes, Aberdeen   oil on canvas   15½ × 23½ in.   signed   (Plate 64)

ADAM BRUCE THOMSON RSA HRSW OBE
(1885–1976)

Adam Bruce Thomson was born in Edinburgh. He studied at the Trustees' Academy, the RGI and then at the newly established ECA where he joined the staff and taught until 1950. During the First World War he served in the Royal Engineers and in 1918 married Jessie Hislop. In 1936 Thomson was elected President of the SSA and in 1946 he became an RSA. The following year he was made a member of the RSW and, in 1968, was made an honorary member. He received his OBE in 1963. Thomson exhibited at the Scottish Gallery in 1946 and, in 1967, at Douglas and Foulis Gallery and the Scottish Arts Club. His work is in numerous public collections including HM the Queen, the SAC and the RSA,

Old Town, Edinburgh, and Arthur's Seat   oil on canvas   27½ × 35½ in.   signed   (Plate 65)

CHARLES FREDERICK TUNNICLIFFE RA
(1901–1979)

Charles Frederick Tunnicliffe was born in the village of Langley near Macclesfield, Cheshire. He grew up on his parents small farm and from an early age displayed an astonishing aptitude for drawing their farm animals. While still at school Tunnicliffe's abilities were discovered by his tutor who managed to get

94

him a scholarship to Macclesfield School of Art from 1915 to 1921, after which he received a scholarship to the RCA. During this time Tunnicliffe's work was still inspired by his love of farm animals and the creatures of the field. At the RCA, having demonstrated his excellent draughtsmanship, Tunnicliffe was directed towards etching. He first became interested in bird life through a meeting with Reginald Wagstaffe, curator of the Stockport Museum and a qualified ornithologist. Tunnicliffe was elected a member of the RA in 1954. There he came to the attention of Sir Alfred Munnings who was so impressed with his engraving of a shire horse that it led to a correspondence between the two men. Tunnicliffe moved from Cheshire to Anglesey, where his studio looked out on to the Cefni estuary, and remained there for the rest of his life. He illustrated more than 80 books including Henry Williamson's *Tarka the Otter*. In addition, Tunnicliffe produced a number of his own books, including *Shoreland Summer Diary* and *My Country Book*.

Red Legged Partridge   watercolour   11 × 15 in.   signed

FRANK WATSON WOOD
(1862–1953)

Frank Wood was born at Berwick on Tweed and studied at Kensington in London and at the Atelier Julian in Paris. He became second master at Newcastle School of Art in 1883 and remained there until 1889. In the same year he was made headmaster at Hawick School of Art, a position he held until 1899. Wood worked mostly in the north, in the Northumberland and Berwickshire areas, and also in Edinburgh, painting marine subjects from 1899. He exhibited his work at the RA, the RSA and the RGI.

Berwick on Tweed   oil on canvas   25 × 30 in.   signed and dated 1908   (Plate 66)

GEORGE WYLLIE
(b. *1921*)

George Wyllie was born in Glasgow and now lives and works in Gourock, Renfrewshire. He was a Customs Officer for all of his working life and received no formal art training. His early sculptures were mainly in metal but he currently uses mixed media. Since 1968 he has had numerous one-man shows including: the MacRobert Centre, University of Stirling; the Talbot Rice Art Centre; the Serpentine Gallery; the Third Eye Centre and the Open Eye Gallery. Wyllie has received several awards including: 1982–3 SAC Travel Award and a British Council Travel Award in 1984. His work can be found in many public collections including: Glasgow Cathedral, the Museum of Transport, Glasgow, the Kelvingrove Museum and Art Gallery, the SAC and the AC.

Glasgow   brass   5ft. high
Bank Balance   wrought iron   10ft. high
Bank Balance   bronze   3ft. 4in. high
Something in the City   wrought iron   5ft. 8in. high

Plate 69 A. YARROW – *Carthorse*

ANNETTE YARROW
(b. *1932*)

Annette Yarrow is the daughter of Scottish parents but was brought up in India. She was educated at Cheltenham and studied nursing at Yorkhill, Glasgow. She had no formal art training and started sculpting in 1966. Since then she has created a large number of bronze figures of horses, wildlife and people, cast by the Morris Singer Foundry in Basingstoke. Annette Yarrow's work is sold through Aspreys of Bond Street. Important private commissions include: *Princess Anne on Doublet*, a life-sized golden eagle on a globe of the world, which forms the Army Air Corps Memorial, and *Badger and Cubs*, which was raffled in aid of the British Wildlife Appeal. Her largest and most important work has been a life-size bronze statue of a bedouin warrior which was commissioned by HM King Hussein of Jordon as a memorial to the 1916 Arab Revolt.

Carthorse bronze 14½ in. high (Plate 69)